HAL•LEONARD®

VIOLIN PLAY-ALONG

AUDIO ACCESS INCLUDED

Bluegrass CLASSICS

Recorded by ABOVE THE TOWN:
Jerry Loughney - Fiddle
Brian Baker - Bass
Bill Brenckle - Guitar
Jon Peik - Banjo

Recorded and Produced by Dan Maske

PLAYBACK+
Speed • Pitch • Balance • Loop

To access audio, visit:
www.halleonard.com/mylibrary

3245-4754-7785-5230

ISBN 978-1-4234-4734-4

HAL•LEONARD®

Visit Hal Leonard Online at
www.halleonard.com

World headquarters, contact:
Hal Leonard
7777 West Bluemound Road
Milwaukee, WI 53213
Email: info@halleonard.com

In Europe, contact:
Hal Leonard Europe Limited
42 Wigmore Street
Marylebone, London, W1U 2RY
Email: info@halleonardeurope.com

In Australia, contact:
Hal Leonard Australia Pty. Ltd.
4 Lentara Court
Cheltenham, Victoria, 3192 Australia
Email: info@halleonard.com.au

Bill Cheatham

Traditional

D.S. al Coda

poco rit.

Blackberry Blossom

Traditional

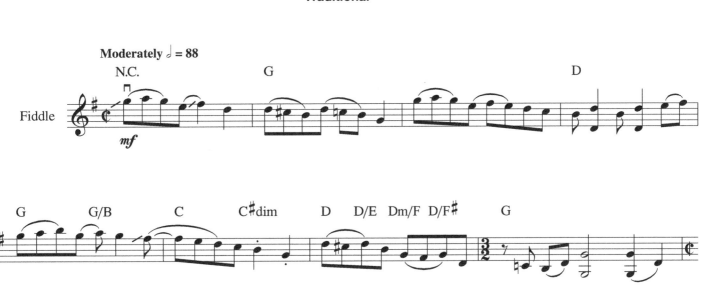

Cripple Creek

American Fiddle Tune

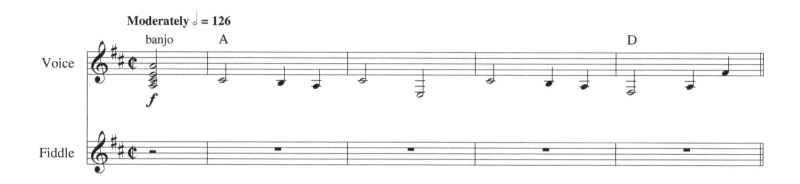

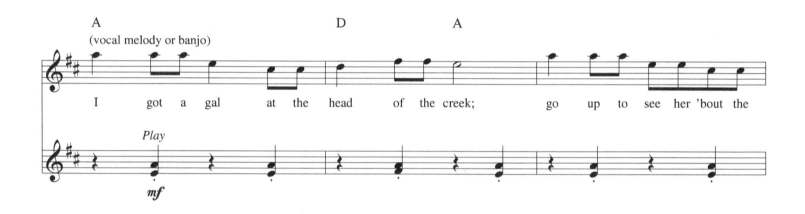

I got a gal at the head of the creek; go up to see her 'bout the

mid - dle of the week. Kiss her on the mouth, just as sweet as an - y wine;

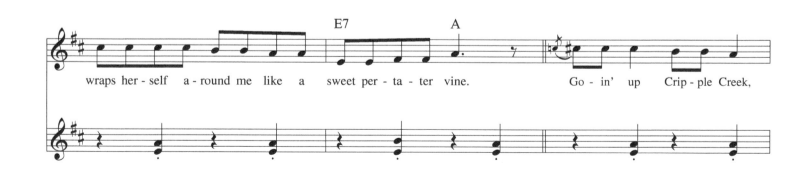

wraps her - self a - round me like a sweet per - ta - ter vine. Go - in' up Crip - ple Creek,

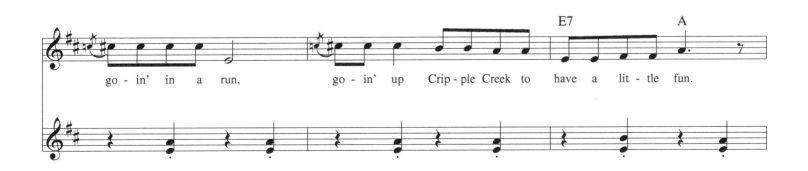

go - in' in a run, go - in' up Crip - ple Creek to have a lit - tle fun.

Go - in' up Crip - ple Creek, go - in' in a whirl, go - in' up Crip - ple Creek to

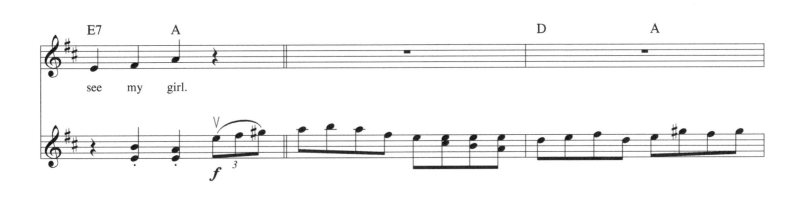

see my girl.

Girls on the Crip - ple Creek 'bout half grown

jump on a boy like a dog on a bone. Roll my britch - es up

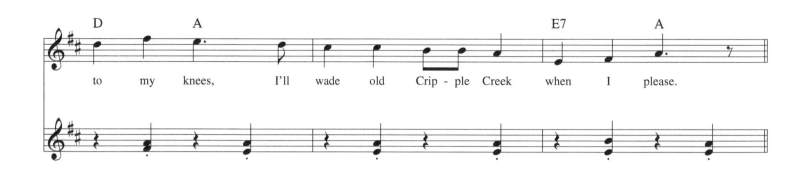

to my knees, I'll wade old Crip - ple Creek when I please.

Go - in' up Crip - ple Creek, go - in' in a run, go - in' up Crip - ple Creek to

have a lit - tle fun. Go - in' up Crip - ple Creek, go - in' in a whirl,

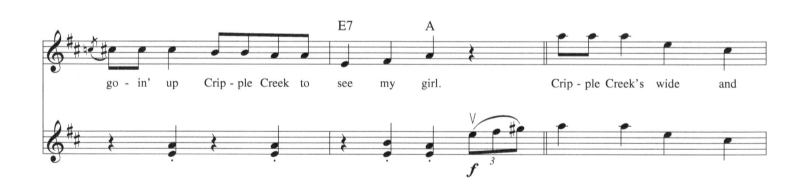

go - in' up Crip - ple Creek to see my girl. Crip - ple Creek's wide and

Crip - ple Creek's deep. I'll wade old Crip - ple Creek a - fore I sleep.

Roads are rock-y and the hill-side's mud-dy and I'm so drunk that I can't stand stead-y. Go-in' up Crip-ple Creek, go-in' in a run, go-in' up Crip-ple Creek to have a lit-tle fun. Go-in' up Crip-ple Creek, go-in' in a whirl, go-in' up Crip-ple Creek to see my girl.

banjo

Great Speckled Bird

Traditional

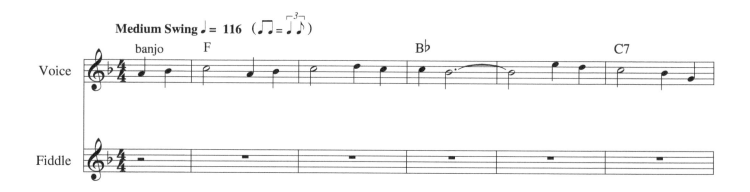

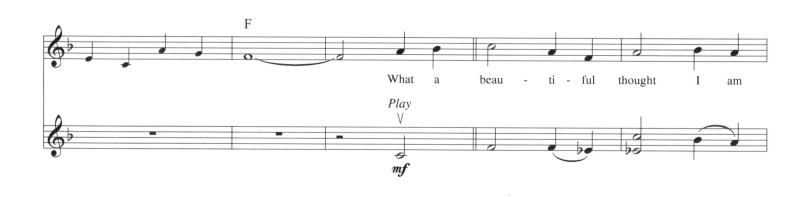

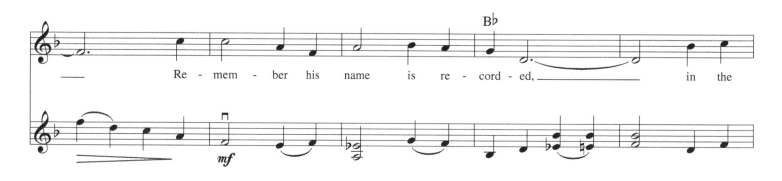

great Book of God's Ho - ly Word. _____ The great speck - led

bird sits in splen - dor, _____ sur - round - ed and de - spised by the

mob. _____ The great speck - led bird is the Bi - ble, _____

_____ re - pre - sent - ing the great Church of God. _____

I am glad that I come to your meet - ing, _____ I'm proud that my name is of a bird. _____ For I want to be one nev - er fear - ing, _____ in the arms of my Sav - ior's true Word. _____ When He

Red Wing

Words by Thurland Chattaway
Music by Kerry Mills

sleep - ing, _____ while Red Wing's weep - ing _____ her heart a -

way.

banjo/vocals

We   watched for him day and   night.   She
There   once lived an In - dian   maid,   a

kept   all the camp - fires   bright.   And   un - der the sky each night she would lie, and
shy   lit - tle prai - rie   maid   who sang a ___ lay, a love song ___ gay, as

dream a - bout his com - ing by and by. But when all the braves re - turned, the
on the plain she'd while a - way the day. She loved a ___ war - rior bold, this

heart of Red Wing yearned,   for far, far a - way her war - ri - or gay fell
shy lit - tle maid of   old.   But brave and ___ gay he rode one ___ day to

brave - ly in ___ the fray. }
bat - tle far ___ a - way. }
Now the moon shines to - night on pret - ty

Red Wing. ___ The breeze is sigh - ing, ___ the night bird's

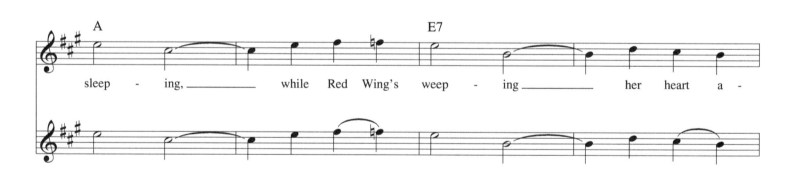

cry - ing. ___ For a - far 'neath his star her brave is

sleep - ing, ___ while Red Wing's weep - ing ___ her heart a -

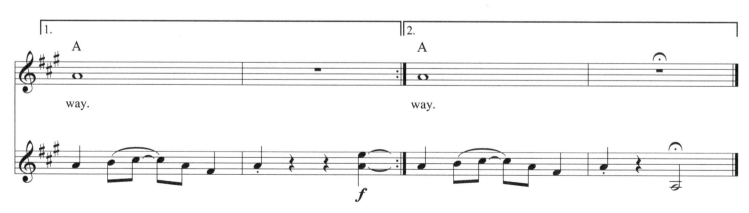

1.

way.

2.

way.

f

Roll in My Sweet Baby's Arms

Traditional

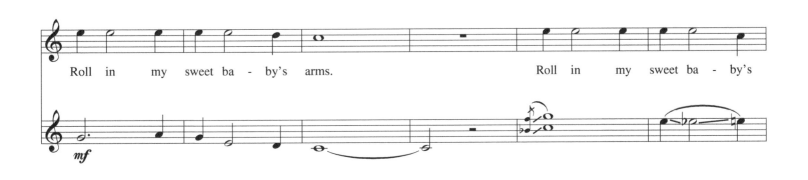

Roll in my sweet ba - by's arms. Roll in my sweet ba - by's

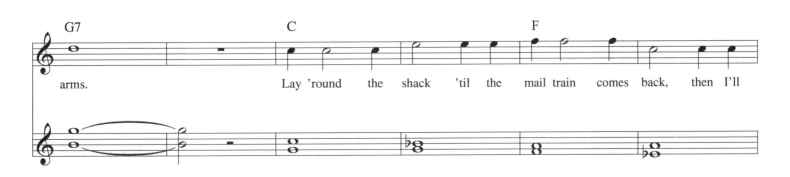

arms. Lay 'round the shack 'til the mail train comes back, then I'll

roll   in   my   sweet   ba-by's   arms.

1. I   ain't gon - na   work   on   the   rail - road,

Ain't gon - na   work on   the   farm,

Lay 'round   the   shack   'til   the   mail train   comes   back,   then   I'll   roll   in   my

sweet ba - by's arms. _____

Roll in my sweet ba - by's arms.

Roll in my sweet ba - by's arms.

Lay 'round the shack 'til the mail train comes back, then I'll roll in my

sweet ba - by's arms. _____

banjo solo

mp

2. Can't see what's the mat - ter with my true love,

she's done quit writ - ing to me, _____ she must think I don't love her like I

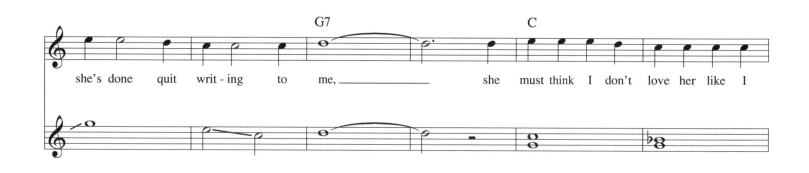

used to, ain't that a fool - ish i - de - a. _____

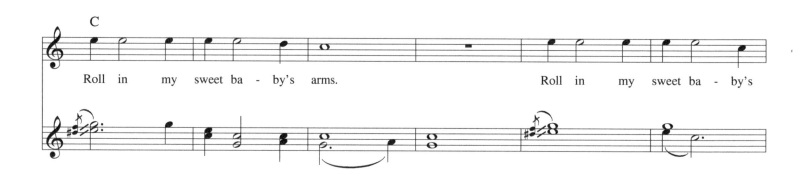

Roll in my sweet ba - by's arms. Roll in my sweet ba - by's

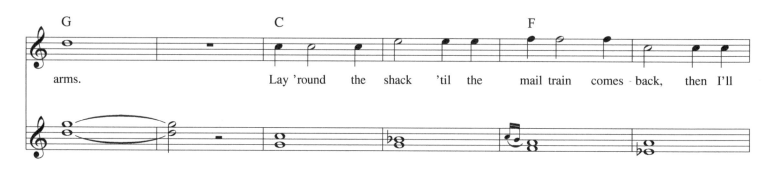

arms. Lay 'round the shack 'til the mail train comes back, then I'll

roll   in   my   sweet   ba - by's   arms. _____

3. Some - times there's   a   change in   the   o - cean, _____   some -

times there's   a   change in   the   sea, _____   some - times there's   a   change   in   my

own __ true __ love,   but there's nev - er   a   change   in __   me. _____

Roll in my sweet ba - by's arms. Roll in my sweet ba - by's

arms. Lay 'round the shack 'til the mail train comes back, then I'll

roll in my sweet ba - by's arms. 4. Ma-ma's a gin-ger - cake

bak - er, Sis - ter can weave and can spin,

Dad's got an int - 'rest in that old cot - ton mill, just watch that old

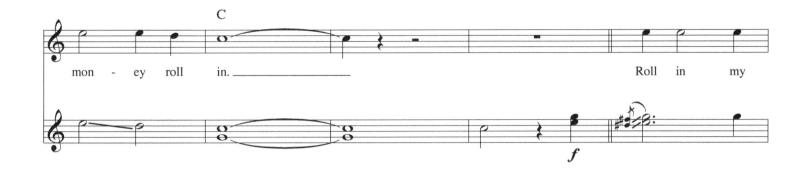

mon - ey roll in. _____ Roll in my

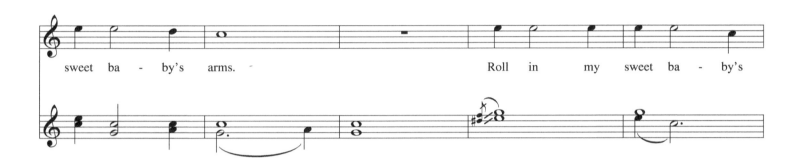

sweet ba - by's arms. Roll in my sweet ba - by's

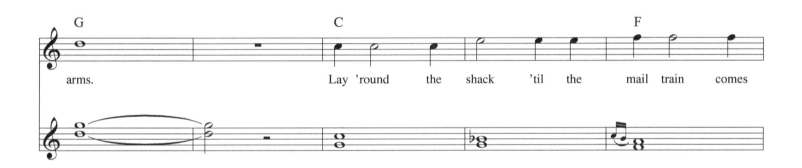

arms. Lay 'round the shack 'til the mail train comes

back, then I'll roll in my sweet ba - by's arms. _____

Additional Verses (optional)

5. They tell me that your parents do not like me,
   They have drove me away from your door.
   If I had all my time to do over,
   I would never go there anymore.

6. Now where was you last Friday night,
   While I was locked up in jail?
   Walking the streets with another man,
   Wouldn't even go my bail.

Turkey in the Straw

American Folksong

Soldier's Joy

Traditional

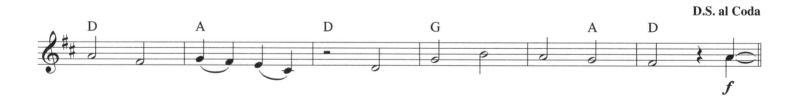